Call the
Ambulance

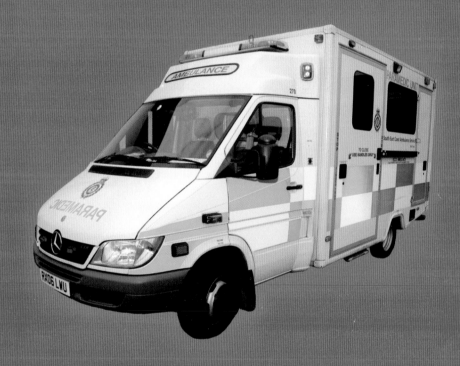

Cath Senker

Photography by Howard Davies

First published in 2010 by
Franklin Watts
338 Euston Road
London NW1 3BH

Franklin Watts Australia
Level 17/207 Kent Street
Sydney NSW 2000

Series editor: Julia Bird

Design: Nimbus Design

Photography: Howard Davies

A CIP catalogue record for this book is available
from the British Library.

ISBN 978 0 7496 9573 6

Dewey classification: 362.1'88

Printed in China

Franklin Watts is a division of Hachette Children's
Books, an Hachette UK company.
www.hachette.co.uk

Acknowledgements

The author and photographer would like to thank
the following for their help in producing this book:
Denise Anderson; Michael Cardona; Esther Cardona
Senker; Abi, Amalia and Elias Cohen; Joe and Finn
Davies; Michelle and Ricky Gibson; Noah, Heff, Joss and
Isaac Lewes; Naomi Marks; Shelley Noronha; Jacky and
Peter Senker.

We would also like to thank the staff of the ambulance
call centre in Lewes, Sussex; Pat Harrington, Ann
Karura, Fionnula Robinson and East Surrey Hospital
Accident and Emergency Department; Rafal
Kowalczyk, Rich Neocleous and all the crews at
Horsham Ambulance Service; Liz Spiers and David
Wells, South East Coast Ambulance Service; Surrey Air
Ambulance Service.

Special thanks to Helena Saarepera from South East
Coast Ambulance Service.

We would also like to thank Surrey Air Ambulance for
providing the photo on p20.

The photos in this book show members of the
emergency services and models. The names of the
models have been changed to protect their privacy.

Cover image: A paramedic drives an ambulance fast,
but safely, to get to an emergency.

Contents

Words in **bold** can be found in the glossary on page 28.

The ambulance team

If someone is ill or has had an accident, the ambulance team are there to help. A caller dials 999 for the ambulance service. A **control centre** worker takes the call. If it's an **emergency**, an ambulance is called. »

The staff at the control centre check the map and work out which ambulance crew to send out.

>> The ambulance crew arrives as fast as possible. **Ambulance technicians** and **paramedics** know how to save lives. They use medical **equipment** and can give out **oxygen** and medicine. Paramedics are more **senior** workers.

Ambulance crew members at Horsham ambulance station in Sussex.

At the ambulance station

Ambulance workers are on hand 24 hours a day. They work **shifts** – either days or nights. Between calls, they may go back to the ambulance station. At the station, they can have something to eat. They also check the ambulance equipment. »

A member of the ambulance crew checks that the **suction unit** is working.

» Ambulance workers have
to keep up their skills.
Sometimes they study
together on the computer.

The ambulance

An ambulance is a truck with many special features. »

siren *makes a loud noise to warn people to keep out of the way*

white light helps the crew find the right house in the dark

blue lights flash to warn traffic to get out of the way

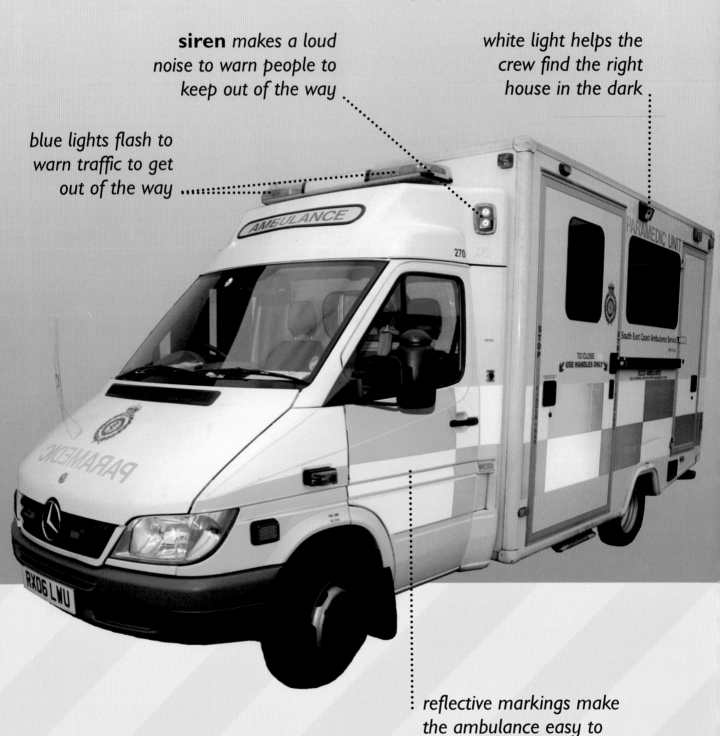

reflective markings make the ambulance easy to spot in the dark

>> There are special features in the driver's cab, too. The crew have a **two-way radio** to speak to the control centre. They can check the address of the emergency on the **sat nav**.

A crew member uses the two-way radio to tell the control centre staff that they are on the way to the hospital.

Inside the ambulance

The ambulance is packed with special medical equipment for treating people in an emergency. »

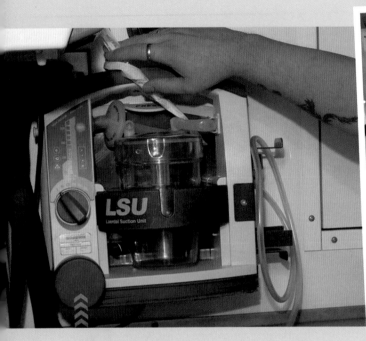

The crew use a suction unit on patients who have something stuck in their throat.

The **stretcher** can be wheeled in and out of the ambulance.

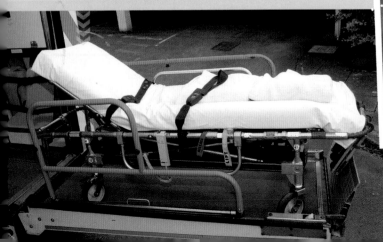

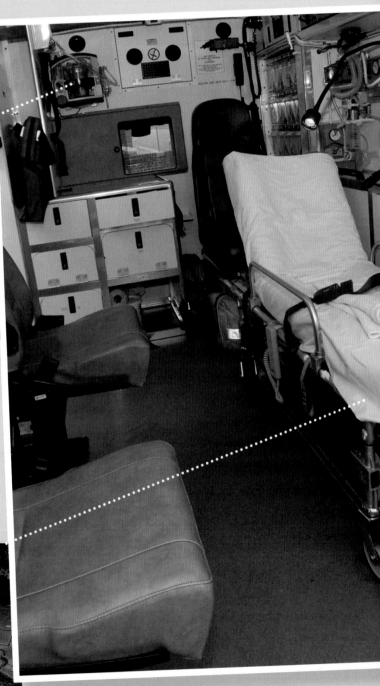

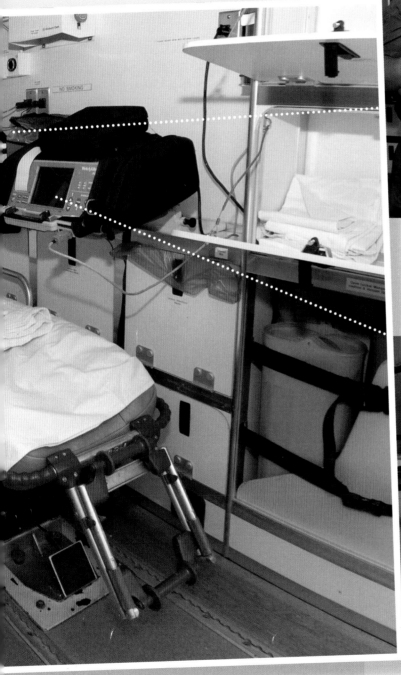

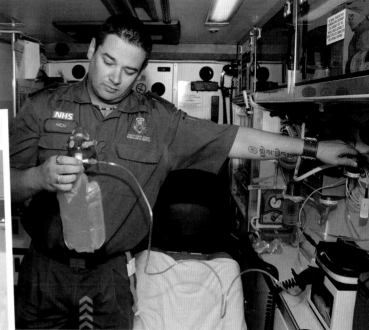

This is an **oxygen unit**. The **mask** goes over the face to help the patient to breathe.

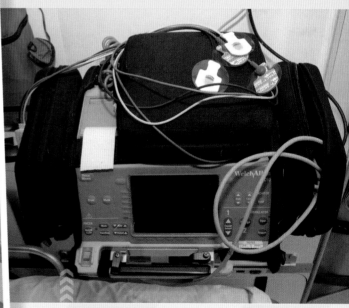

A **defibrillator** or 'shock box' starts a patient's heart again if it has stopped.

Training

To train to be a paramedic, you need to be fit, healthy and strong. It takes at least three years to train for the job.

Student paramedics study the human body, illness and how to make people better. They also learn to drive fast, but safely, in an emergency. »

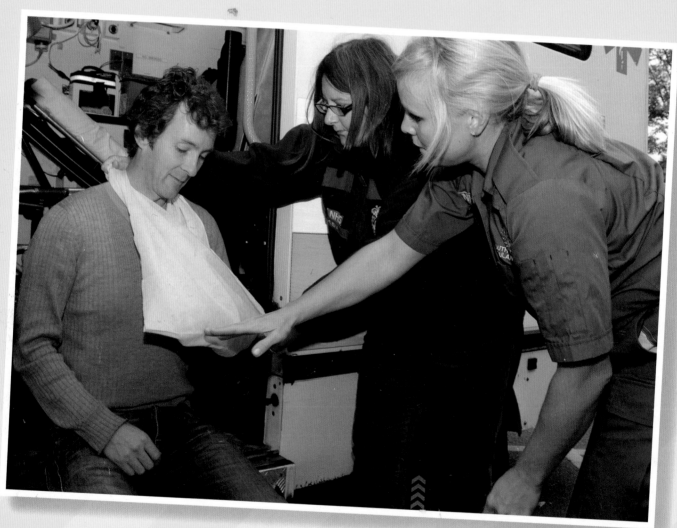

A paramedic shows a student paramedic how to put a patient's arm in a **sling**.

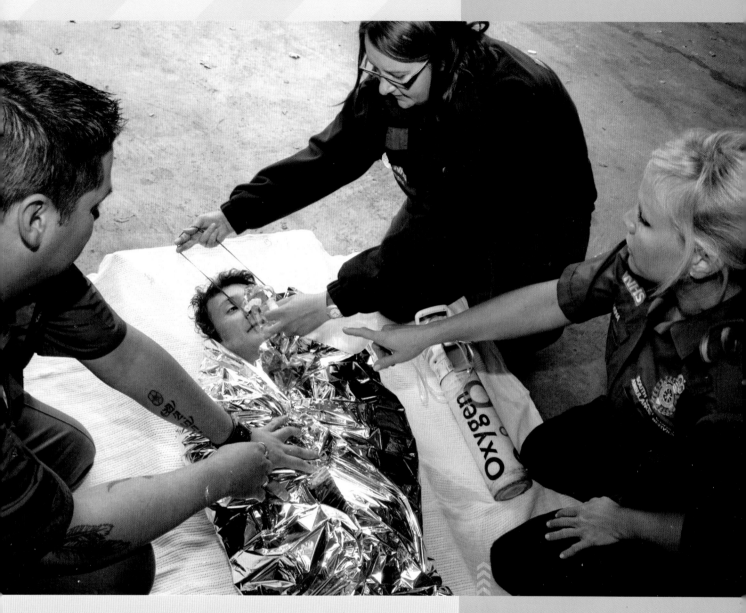

The crew show the student paramedic how to wrap a patient in a **foil blanket** to keep him warm. She practises placing a mask over his face.

>> To become a paramedic you have to go to university. Student paramedics are taught to work out quickly what has happened to a patient. They learn how to treat people who have had accidents, burns, **heart attacks** and falls.

Rapid response!

After picking up a 999 call, the control centre worker calls the ambulance station. A crew of two prepare to leave as quickly as possible. »

The crew stop what they are doing. They hurry into the ambulance within 30 seconds!

Ambulance drivers have special blue light training to learn how to drive safely at high speed.

>> The ambulance drives at great speed. The siren blares and the blue lights flash. Cars have to move out of the way to let the ambulance pass.

Heart attack

Sarah has had a heart attack. Her husband calls an ambulance and the crew arrive quickly at the emergency. »

Sarah has had a heart attack in her garden.

» The ambulance crew have to work quickly. If Sarah is not treated straight away, she will die. »

One ambulance worker presses down on Sarah's chest to keep her heart beating. The other gets the defibrillator ready.

» They use the defibrillator to give Sarah an electric shock. It makes her heart start working again. Then they take her to hospital where she may have an **operation**.

Road accident

Several cars have crashed in a road accident. The air ambulance has been called. It's quicker to take badly hurt patients to hospital by helicopter than by ambulance. **»**

Helicopters can travel faster than ambulances so are useful in an emergency.

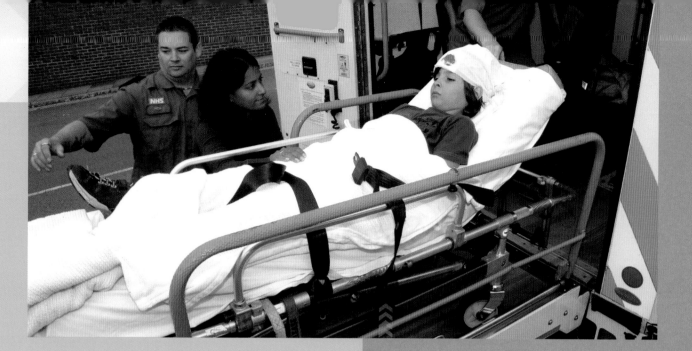

Jacob is wheeled into the ambulance on a stretcher.

>> Jacob was in the accident. He is not badly hurt, so he can go in an ordinary ambulance. The crew put him on a stretcher to keep him still in case he has broken any bones.

Jacob has cut his head. The ambulance crew bandage the cut to slow down the bleeding.

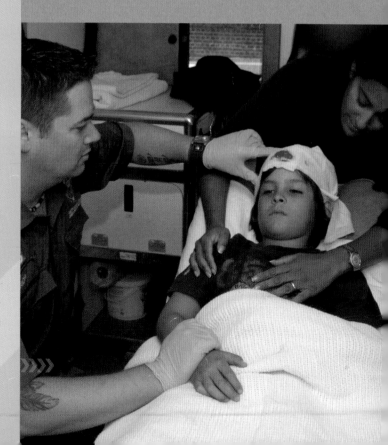

Inside the ambulance, a crew member checks the bleeding. Jacob is then taken to the hospital.

Emergencies at home

Accidents often happen at home. People may fall over. If they are very elderly, they may not be able to get up by themselves.

Sometimes people fall off ladders or chairs while they are working in the house. »

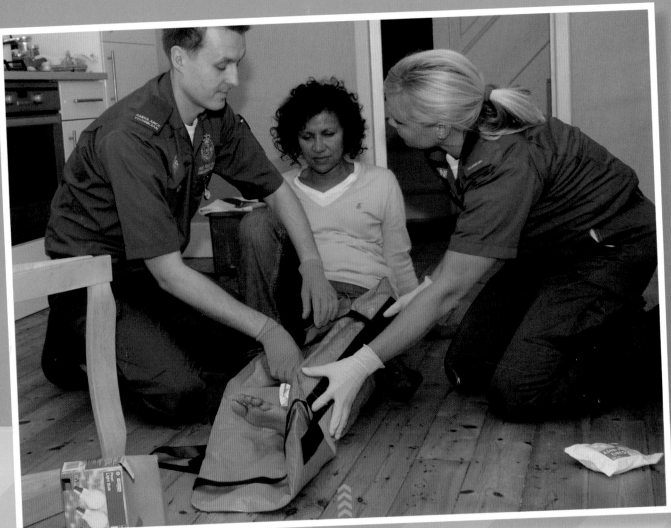

This woman fell and broke her leg. The crew wrap her leg in a **vacuum splint** to keep it still.

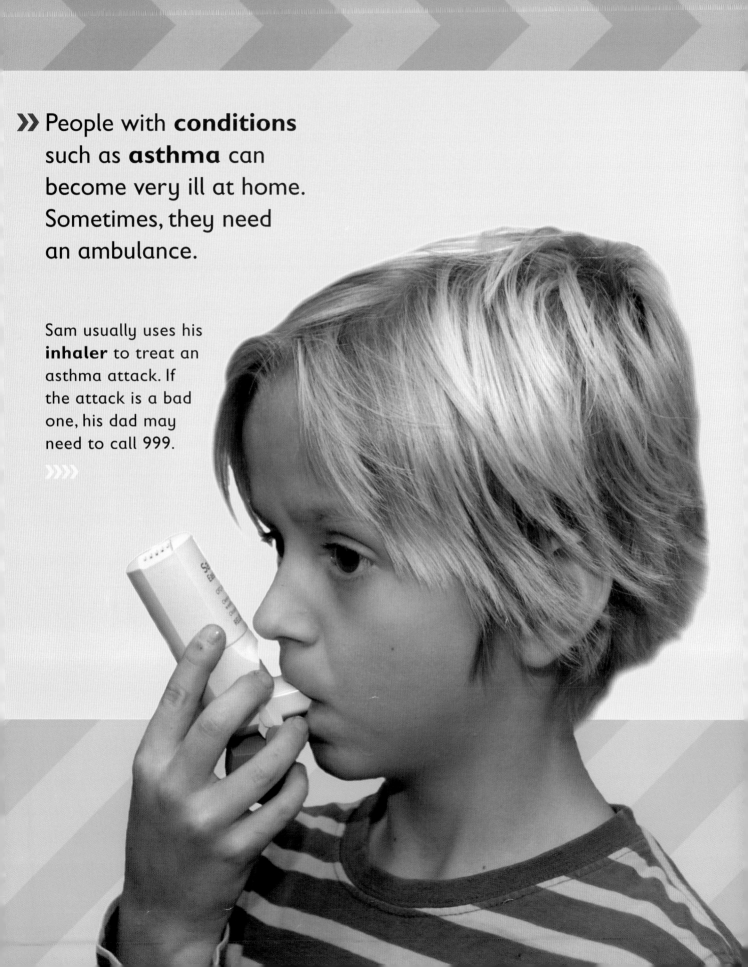

» People with **conditions** such as **asthma** can become very ill at home. Sometimes, they need an ambulance.

Sam usually uses his **inhaler** to treat an asthma attack. If the attack is a bad one, his dad may need to call 999.

»»»

Going to hospital

Sam's asthma attack is too bad for the inhaler to treat. The paramedics do what they can for him at home. Then they take him to hospital for more treatment. »

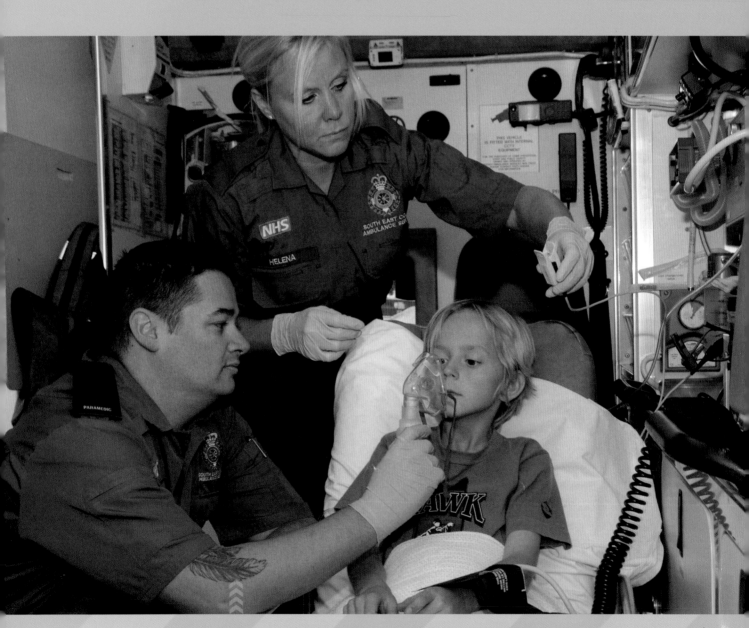

Before leaving for the hospital, the crew place an oxygen mask over Sam's face to help him breathe.

>> The ambulance arrives at hospital. The crew quickly take Sam in on a stretcher. >>

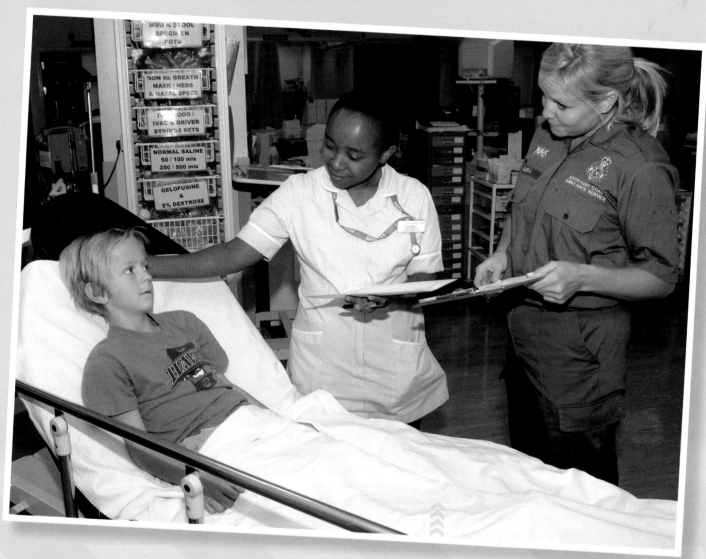

The paramedic explains to the nurse what has happened.

>> A doctor sees Sam and says he will be fine after some more treatment. Sam will be allowed to go home tomorrow.

Keep safe!

You can avoid accidents at home in simple ways.

Be safe with **electricity**. Switch off items like TVs and computers when you're not using them. Make sure people can't trip over the leads. »

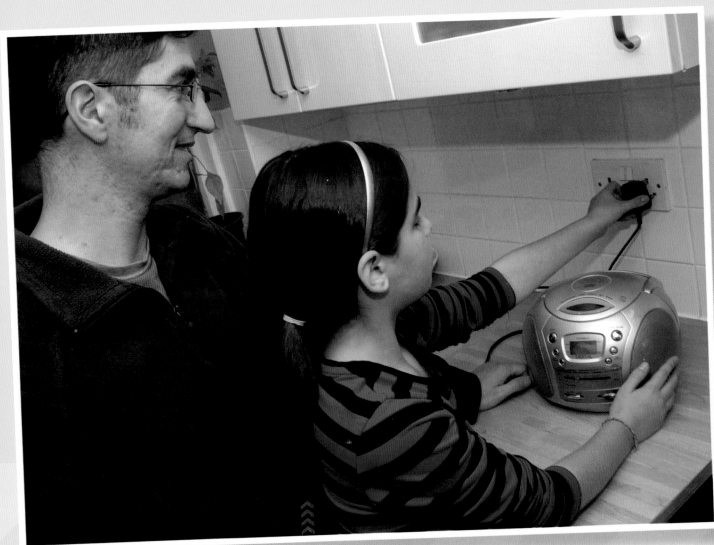

The switch should be off when you plug in a CD player. Plug sockets have electricity in them. Electricity can hurt you. Ask an adult to help you to plug in electrical items.

>> In the kitchen, keep away from the hot cooker and boiling water.

If you're cooking, keep the pan handle to the side. Always ask an adult to help you.

>> Keep safe when you're out and about. Wear a helmet when you go out on your bike or scooter. >>

A cycle helmet protects your head if you fall off.

27

Glossary

ambulance technician
A person who works with a paramedic. He or she drives the ambulance and helps to save people's lives.

asthma
A condition that makes it hard to breathe.

condition
When something is wrong with your body.

control centre
A place where people take 999 calls.

defibrillator
A machine that gives an electric shock to the heart.

electricity
A form of energy that is used to give power, light and heat. Electricity can be very dangerous if it is not used with care.

emergency
A serious situation that happens suddenly and needs immediate attention.

equipment
Tools and machines that are designed to do a particular job.

foil blanket
A blanket used in an emergency to keep a person warm.

heart attack
Sudden heart disease, when too little blood reaches the heart.

inhaler
A device for breathing in medicine.

operation
When doctors use tools to work on a patient's body.

oxygen
A gas in the air that people need to breathe.

oxygen mask
A mask that covers the nose and mouth and allows you to breathe oxygen.

oxygen unit
A device with a tank of oxygen and a mask for the patient.

paramedic
A senior ambulance worker who uses special equipment to save lives.

sat nav
A device that shows you exactly where you are. It uses a signal from a satellite that orbits (goes around) the Earth.

senior
High in rank.

shift
A shift is the time that a person works, for example, from 7 p.m. to 7 a.m.

siren
A device that makes a loud warning sound.

sling
A bandage hanging from the neck to support a hand or arm.

stretcher
A device like a cot for carrying an injured person.

suction unit
A device that sucks objects or liquid from a person's throat.

two-way radio
A radio for sending and receiving messages.

vacuum splint
A padded wrapping used to protect an injured body part.

Finding out more

Books

Ambulance Crew by Clare Oliver (Franklin Watts, 2007)

Ambulances by Gary M. Amoroso and Cynthia Klingel
(Child's World, 2007)

In the Ambulance Service by Ruth Thomson (Wayland, 2008)

Paramedic by Sue Barraclough (Franklin Watts, 2005)

Paramedic by Rebecca Hunter (Cherrytree, 2006)

Websites

British Red Cross Children First Aid
http://childrenfirstaid.redcross.org.uk/
How to carry out emergency first aid – with videos,
animations and quizzes.

Children's, Youth and Women's Health Service – Your Health
http://www.cyh.com/HealthTopics/HealthTopicCategories.aspx?p=285
Links to first aid for bleeding, broken bones, burns and people
who are badly hurt.

Easy health
http://www.easyhealth.org.uk/callinganambulance.aspx
How to call an ambulance and links to simple information
about the health service.

Safe Kids Activities for Kids
http://www.safekids.co.uk/SafetyActivitiesCategory.html
Posters with safety messages to colour in.

Note to parents and teachers: every effort has been made by the Publishers to
ensure that these websites are suitable for children, that they are of the highest
educational value, and that they contain no inappropriate or offensive material.
However, because of the nature of the Internet, it is impossible to guarantee that
the contents of these sites will not be altered. We strongly advise that Internet
access is supervised by a responsible adult.

Index